SOMETHING FOR THE GIRLS

Seventeen smash hit songs arranged for piano, voice and guitar

CONTENTS

Published 2003
© International Music Publications Limited
Griffin House 161 Hammersmith Road London England W6 8BS

Project management Artemis Music Limited

Can't Get You Out Of My Head

Words and Music by Cathy Dennis and Robert Davis

Come Away With Me

Words and Music by Norah Jones

Fallin'

Words and Music by Alicia Augello-Cook

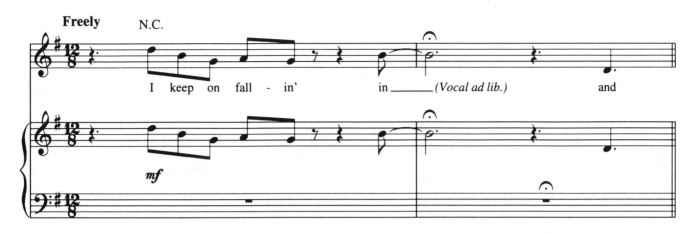

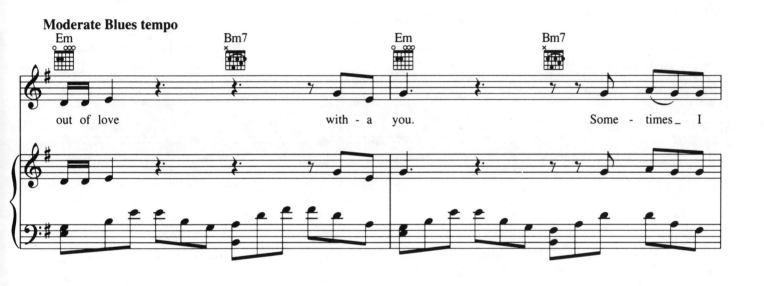

love with - a you. I _____ nev - er loved some - one _____ the way that

I love a - you. I'm _____ fall - in' in and out _____ of

love with - a you. I _____ nev - er loved some - one _____ the way that

I love a - you. I'm _____ fall - in' in and out _____ of

Complicated

Words and Music by Lauren Christy, David Alspach, Graham Edwards and Avril Lavigne

And if you could on - ly let it be,___ you will see___
Where you are ain't where___ it's at. You see,___ you're mak - ing me___

...end solo)

I like you the way___ you are when we're driv - ing in___ your car
laugh out when you strike___ your pose. Take off all your prep - py clothes.
Chill out, what - cha yell - ing for? Lay back, it's all been done___ be - fore.

and you're talk - ing to___ me one on one.___ But you be - come___
You know you're not fool - ing an - y - one___ when you be - come___
And if you could on - ly let it be,_____ you will see___

Dilemma

Words and Music by Kenneth Gamble, Bunny Sigler, Cornell Haynes and Antoine Macone

Gm7   C   Am7   Dm

when I'm with__ my boo,__ boy, you know I'm cra-zy o-ver you.__ No

Gm7   C   Am7   Dm

mat-ter what__ I do,_____ all I think a-bout__ is you.__ E-ven

Gm7   C   Am7   Dm

when I'm with__ my boo,__ you know I'm cra-zy o-ver you.__

Verse:

Gm7   C

(Nelly:)

1. I met this chick and she just moved right up the block from me, and
2. *See additional lyrics*

Verse 2:
I see a lot and you look and I never say a word.
I know how niggaz start actin' trippin' out here about they girls.
And there's no way Nelly gon' fight over no dame, as you could see.
But I like your steez, your style, your whole demeanor.
The way you come through and holla and swoop me in his two-seater.
Now that's gangstah and I got special ways to thank ya.
Don't you forget it but, it ain't that easy for you to pack up and leave him.
But you and dirty got ties for different reasons.
I respect that and right before I turn to leave, she said,
"You don't know what you mean to me."
(To Chorus:)

Family Portrait

Words and Music by Alecia Moore and Scott Storch

I Don't Want To Miss A Thing

Words and Music by Diane Warren

40

Repeat ad lib. and fade

Genie In A Bottle

Words and Music by Pam Sheyne, David Frank and Steve Kipner

How Do I Live

Words and Music by Diane Warren

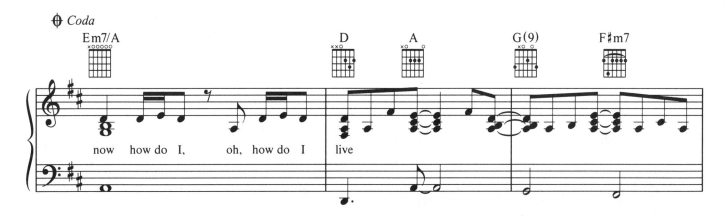

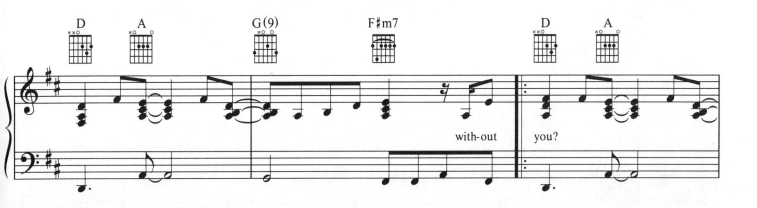

Repeat ad lib. and fade
(vocal 1st time only)

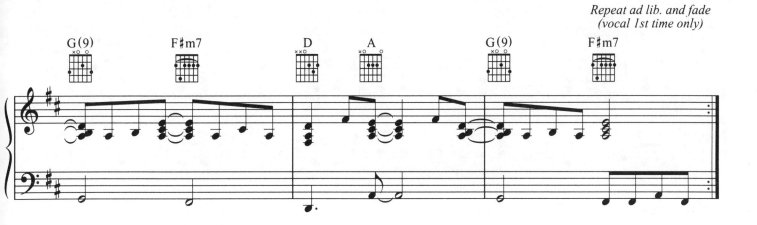

Verse 2:
Without you, there'd be no sun in my sky,
There would be no love in my life,
There'd be no world left for me.
And I, baby, I don't know what I would do,
I'd be lost if I lost you.
If you ever leave,
Baby, you would take away everything real in my life.
And tell me now...
(To Chorus:)

I Love Rock 'n' Roll

Words and Music by Alan Merrill and Jake Hooker

(Spoken): Hey, is this thing on?

1. I

(1.) saw him danc-ing there___ by the re-cord ma-chine.
(2.) smiled so I got up___ and asked for his name.

I

"But

58

I'm Like A Bird

Words and Music by Nelly Furtado

64

Just A Little

Words and Music by Michelle Escoffery, John Hammond-Hagan and George Hammond-Hagan

Ah. — Yeah, — yeah. Mm.

1. Sex — y, ev — 'ry — thing a — bout you's so sex — y.
2. Let me, I do a — ny — thing if you just let me.

You don't ev — en know what you got. ——— You're real — ly hit — ting my spot. —
Find a way to make you respond. I know you wan — na break down those

My Heart Will Go On

Words by Will Jennings
Music by James Horner

76

Sound Of The Underground

Words and Music by Brian Higgins, Niara Scarlett and Miranda Cooper

1. Dis - co danc - ing with the lights down low.
2. Chain re - ac - tion run-ning through my veins.

Beats are pump - ing on my ste - re - o.
Pumps still rac - ing up in - to my brain.

Then you see me ov - er - flow, where the girls get down with the sound on the ra - di - o.

Out to the 'lec - tric night, where the bass line jumps to the back - street light. The

To Coda ⊕

beat goes a - round and round, it's the sound of the un - der, sound of the un - der -

1.

Synth. N.C.

- ground.

Thank You

Words and Music by Dido Armstrong and Paul Herman

Verse 2:
I drank too much last night, got bills to pay,
My head just feels in pain.
I missed the bus and there'll be hell today,
I'm late for work again.
And even if I'm there, they'll all imply
That I might not last the day.
And then you call me and it's not so bad, it's not so bad.
(To Chorus:)

Whole Again

Words and Music by Stuart Kershaw, Andy McCluskey, Bill Padley and Jeremy Godfrey

Stronger

Words and Music by Jony Rockstar, Marius De Vries, Felix Howard,
Mutya Buena, Keisha Buchanan and Heidi Range

1. I'll make it through the rai - ny days,⎯ I'll be the one
2. Some-times I feel so down⎯ and out,⎯ like e - mo -

⎯ who stands⎯ here long - er than⎯ the rest.⎯ When my land-
-tion that's⎯ been cap - tured in⎯ a maze. I had my